Daily Fix 5 A Day Copyright © 2018 by Richard Akita

Richard Akita
P.O. BOX CT11163,
Cantonments
Accra, Ghana
Alternatively, visit www.richardakita.com

Ordering Information:
Quantity sales. Special discounts are available on quantity purchases by corporations, churches, schools, associations and others. For details, contact the publisher at the address above, Email or call.

E-mail:
info@richardakita.com
Call: 0263 260 101

Printed by Launchpad Press
First Printing, 2018

Cover designed by Ryzard Akita
Editing and typesetting by Launchpad Press

Dedication
My mum; Mrs Florence Dedei Akita

INTRODUCTION

Every year as we celebrate the gift of an additional year, it stirs up moments of introspection.

- How well did we use our time?
- What opportunities did I maximise or waste?
- What is my relevance?
- What is my legacy?

The questions are not limited to the above but varies and are personal.

I do not claim to know it all, on the contrary I have taken painful lessons from both my failures and successes with the hope it will inspire you to action.

Planning your life in small bitesize chalks the very victory you desire, as you review your efforts, recalibrate and launch your next strategic step of action.

Your existence in this time space must be meaningful and hopefully cause you to be legacy minded as your actions and victories benefit someone.

As a catalyst, I simply by daring my reader to engage their life at the helm, stir up dormant gifts and soar in the area of influence.

Daily fix, is a bitesize workbook that necessitates your full commitment, requiring larruping of previous disappointments or leveraging previous successes.

Crafted victory
is never for the
lazy
#Richardakita
richardakita
akitarichard
www.richardakita.com

I Walked!

I walked this earth; toiled, battered, failed and won a few.

I walked this earth; focusing on the few, did change my sight.

Understanding your purpose cushions, the knocks.

Life questions your purpose; your response demands more answers.

I still can make a difference by "daydoing" and not daydreaming.

My focused actions will leave my footprint and cause a ripple effect as I refuse to be a cunctator.

I walked this earth.

Richard Akita

How 1 daily action leads to success;

Einstein is reputed to have said that insanity *is 'doing the same thing repeatedly and expecting different results'*. Therein lies a very valuable lesson for goal achievement. You cannot sit back waiting for things to happen for you.

If you have set a major goal, it is because you want something to change in your life. If you want something to change; you must change something.

It is easy to be overwhelmed by the size of a new goal. When viewed as a whole, it can seem daunting and unachievable. The key to achieving such goals is to break them down into bite size chunks. That way, you can take daily action to help bring you closer to the goal. When you focus on daily action, you can move closer to your objective, one step at a time, without being distracted by the enormity of the task.

Daily action is the silver bullet

When you see people achieve great success, it is tempting to believe that there was one big thing which they did to achieve that success. You may then set about trying to discover what that silver bullet was.

Everybody wants to be successful, but not so many want to accept that success is achieved by hard work rather than one specific act.

In his book *'Slaying the Dragon: How to Turn Your Small Steps to Great Feats'*; American sprinter Michael Johnson discusses the trials and tribulations which he endured on his path to becoming an athletics legend. He discusses the winning mentality he developed and how he had to deal with setbacks on his way to glory. Johnson had worked for years to give himself the best opportunity for success at the 1992 Olympics in Barcelona. Unfortunately, it did not go to plan. Rather than feel sorry for himself, Johnson identified the daily actions which he could take to recover from the setback. In 1996, at the Atlanta Olympics, Johnson wrote his name into the history books as one of the greatest, if not the greatest, 200 & 400 metre runners of all time. It wasn't one big act which ensured Johnson's place in history; it was his focus on daily action.

Daily action is consistent and persistent

When Jack Canfield and Mark Victor Hansen wrote their first *'Chicken Soup for the Soul: Stories to Open the Heart and Rekindle the Spirit'* book, they sought a great deal of advice on how best to market the book. In 'The Success Principles(TM): How to Get from Where You Are to Where You Want to Be' Canfield tells how they settled on 'the rule of 5'. This meant that every day they did 5 things to promote the book. Some of the examples which Canfield provides include:

- 5 Radio interviews
- Send a copy to 5 book reviewers
- Send a copy to 5 celebrities

These were all simple things to do but over time they add up. It took over a year but eventually 'Chicken Soup for the Soul' began to appear on the best sellers list. It was all down to Mark and Jack's focus on daily actions.

The term, 'overnight success' is used too often and is rarely accurate. There are very few people who achieve success quickly, due to one or two actions. Those who do achieve success quickly rarely hold onto that success. In reality, the old saying *'It takes a long time to become an overnight success'* is true. A lot of work goes into achieving a major goal.

Much of this work goes unnoticed but without it, success would not be possible.

The most successful people have big goals, but they know that if they are to achieve these goals, they need to turn them into daily action which they can take to bring them closer to the goal.

At the end of each day, ask yourself one question 'What action can I take tomorrow to bring me closer to that goal?' The answer will be your daily action. Schedule that action and make sure that action is completed. You will soon be progressing toward your goal.

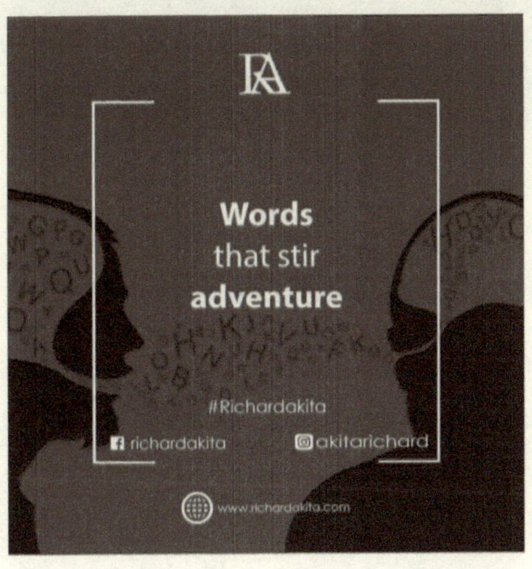

The Daily Goal Setting Worksheet

A day goal setting worksheet is more than just a bucket list of what you want to do in your life. It is a road map of how to get there!

Whether you are setting personal or work goals, a worksheet makes it more likely that you will achieve what you are aiming for.

There are 3 main reasons why you should use a daily goal worksheet;

1. Putting ink to paper on a goal setting worksheet transforms your goals from the abstract to the real. It creates a bridge between today's dreams and tomorrow's reality

2. A worksheet helps to plan and brainstorm strategies to set goals, and

3. You can easily track and update your progress

"Without goals, and plans to reach them, you are like a ship that has set sail with no destination". ~ Fitzhugh Dodson

Using the daily Goal Setting Worksheet

A consistent daily action gets you to your desired destination, therefore, think about those things that you want to achieve today.

Maybe you want to be in better shape, be more productive in your work, have better relationships. What daily small, yet practical action can you practice bringing it into fruition?

Step 1: Read the Life Lesson

The daily fix is only a catalyst, yet a thought provoking quote that demands an action.

Step 2: What is your interpretation of the Fix?

After reading the daily fix, where appropriate write down your interpretation.

Step 3: List your daily goals.

List no more than 5 goals on your worksheet in present tense as though they have already happened.

Step 4: List your supporting 5 actions

For each of your goals see if you can list 5 actions that will be used to support your goal.

For example;

I look back over my ongoing goal to be *"in the best shape I have been."*

These are my daily action:

- to walk to the local shop rather than use the car
- to cook, eat health food, eat dinner before 5:30pm and no snacking after 6pm
- to eat at least 5 fruits daily
- to find an accountability partner
- to meditate at least 5 minutes' daily

So, what is it that you want to accomplish with your daily action plan? Write down your goal and follow them up with a plan of 5 actions.

Don't just use it for personal goals - also look to use it for work goals.

Step 5: Review your day, "What was the outcome"

RA

Your actions, not your words, are ultimately what truly matters.

Richard AKITA
One life, make it count

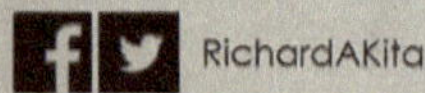 RichardAKita 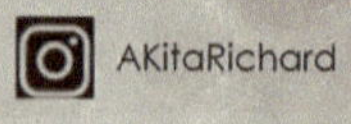 AKitaRichard 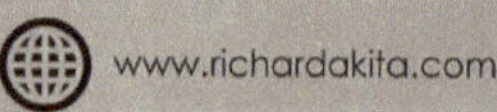 www.richardakita.com

image: pixabay.com

Daily Fix:

The sound of wind sometimes announces the rain just as pain in our body announces a malfunction.

2. Your view: ____

____

____

____

3. Daily goals:

- ____

- ____

- ____

- ____

- ____

4. Supporting action:

- ____

- ____

- ____

- ____

- ____

5 Review:

- ____

- ____

- ____

- ____

- ____

Daily fix:

Thinking you are knowledgeable does not make you wise, just as believing you are correct only feeds your ego.

2. Your view: _______________________________

____

____

____

3. Daily goals:

- _______________________________
- _______________________________
- _______________________________
- _______________________________
- _______________________________

4. Supporting action:

- _______________________________
- _______________________________
- _______________________________
- _______________________________
- _______________________________

5 Review:

- _______________________________
- _______________________________
- _______________________________
- _______________________________
- _______________________________

Daily fix:

Noise is not always the sound of victory but alert. Love is never about emotions but a decision. Don't get knicker twisted.

2. Your view: _______________________________

____

____

____

3. Daily goals:

- _______________________________________
- _______________________________________
- _______________________________________
- _______________________________________
- _______________________________________

4. Supporting action:

- _______________________________________
- _______________________________________
- _______________________________________
- _______________________________________
- _______________________________________

5 Review:

- _______________________________________
- _______________________________________
- _______________________________________
- _______________________________________
- _______________________________________

Daily fix:

OPULENCE!!
Frugal, generous or impulsive? Life is like a coin. You can spend it on anything, but only ONCE.

2. Your view: _______________________________

____

____

____

3. Daily goals:

- _______________________________
- _______________________________
- _______________________________
- _______________________________
- _______________________________

4. Supporting action:

- _______________________________
- _______________________________
- _______________________________
- _______________________________
- _______________________________

5 Review:

- _______________________________
- _______________________________
- _______________________________
- _______________________________
- _______________________________

Daily fix:

"If you bring forth what is within you, what is within you will save you. If you don't bring forth what is within you, what is within you will destroy you." – Jodi Picoult

2. Your view: _______________________________

____

____

____

3. Daily goals:

- _______________________________
- _______________________________
- _______________________________
- _______________________________
- _______________________________

4. Supporting action:

- _______________________________
- _______________________________
- _______________________________
- _______________________________
- _______________________________

5 Review:

- _______________________________
- _______________________________
- _______________________________
- _______________________________
- _______________________________

Daily fix:

"What seems to us as bitter trials are often blessings in disguise." – Oscar Wilde

2. Your view: _______________________________

____

____

____

3. Daily goals:

- ____
- ____
- ____
- ____
- ____

4. Supporting action:

- ____
- ____
- ____
- ____
- ____

5 Review:

- ____
- ____
- ____
- ____
- ____

Daily fix:

'If you are not willing to risk the usual you will have to settle for the ordinary." – Jim Rohn

2. Your view: _______________________________

____

____

____

3. Daily goals:

- _______________________________
- _______________________________
- _______________________________
- _______________________________
- _______________________________

4. Supporting action:

- _______________________________
- _______________________________
- _______________________________
- _______________________________
- _______________________________

5 Review:

- _______________________________
- _______________________________
- _______________________________
- _______________________________
- _______________________________

Daily fix:

"Any change, even a change for the better, is always accompanied by drawbacks and discomforts." – Arnold Bennett

2. Your view: _______________________________

____

____

____

3. Daily goals:

- _______________________________
- _______________________________
- _______________________________
- _______________________________
- _______________________________

4. Supporting action:

- _______________________________
- _______________________________
- _______________________________
- _______________________________
- _______________________________

5 Review:

- _______________________________
- _______________________________
- _______________________________
- _______________________________

Daily fix:

"Mistakes are a great educator when one is honest enough to admit them and willing to learn from them." – Alexander Solzhenitsyn

2. Your view: _______________________________

____

____

____

3. Daily goals:

- ____
- ____
- ____
- ____
- ____

4. Supporting action:

- ____
- ____
- ____
- ____
- ____

5 Review:

- ____
- ____
- ____
- ____
- ____

Daily fix:

Happiness is oversubscribed. There are vacancies at endurance and perseverance. Apply within!

2. Your view: _______________________

____

____

____

3. Daily goals:

- _______________________
- _______________________
- _______________________
- _______________________
- _______________________

4. Supporting action:

- _______________________
- _______________________
- _______________________
- _______________________
- _______________________

5 Review:

- _______________________
- _______________________
- _______________________
- _______________________
- _______________________

Daily fix:

Mic Check!! Your consistent action is your unspoken voice. Be conscious of your voice.

2. Your view: _______________________

____

____

____

3. Daily goals:

- _____________________________________
- _____________________________________
- _____________________________________
- _____________________________________
- _____________________________________

4. Supporting action:

- _____________________________________
- _____________________________________
- _____________________________________
- _____________________________________
- _____________________________________

5 Review:

- _____________________________________
- _____________________________________
- _____________________________________
- _____________________________________
- _____________________________________

Daily fix:

Everything that last, remains constant, endures the test of time, has been a high cost to someone who dared to pay the price. Will you pay the price for another to enjoy?

2. Your view: _______________________________

____

____

____

3. Daily goals:

- ____
- ____
- ____
- ____
- ____

4. Supporting action:

- ____
- ____
- ____
- ____
- ____

5 Review:

- ____
- ____
- ____
- ____
- ____

Daily fix:

The difference between try and triumph is a little oomph.

2. Your view: __________________________________

____

____

____

3. Daily goals:

- ____

- ____

- ____

- ____

- ____

4. Supporting action:

- ____

- ____

- ____

- ____

- ____

5 Review:

- ____

- ____

- ____

- ____

- ____

Daily fix:

Promise the ordinary and deliver the extraordinary.

2. Your view: _______________________________

____

____

____

3. Daily goals:

- ____
- ____
- ____
- ____
- ____

4. Supporting action:

- ____
- ____
- ____
- ____
- ____

5 Review:

- ____
- ____
- ____
- ____

Daily fix:

Why not intimidate the challenges facing you by turning them into learning opportunities?

2. Your view: _______________________________

____

____

____

3. Daily goals:

- ____
- ____
- ____
- ____
- ____

4. Supporting action:

- ____
- ____
- ____
- ____
- ____

5 Review:

- ____
- ____
- ____
- ____
- ____

Daily fix:

Be hungry for more; unlike Oliver Twist; yours should be information not food.

2. Your view: _______________________________

____

____

____

3. Daily goals:

- _______________________________
- _______________________________
- _______________________________
- _______________________________
- _______________________________

4. Supporting action:

- _______________________________
- _______________________________
- _______________________________
- _______________________________
- _______________________________

5 Review:

- _______________________________
- _______________________________
- _______________________________
- _______________________________
- _______________________________

Daily fix:

The sound of victory is quieter than the noise of failure yet its failure that announces victory.

2. Your view: ________________________________

____

____

____

3. Daily goals:

- ____
- ____
- ____
- ____
- ____

4. Supporting action:

- ____
- ____
- ____
- ____
- ____

5 Review:

- ____
- ____
- ____
- ____
- ____

Daily fix:

We are born originals but apparently some die as copies. What original act will you perform today to impact others?

2. Your view: _______________________________

____

____

____

3. Daily goals:

- ____
- ____
- ____
- ____
- ____

4. Supporting action:

- ____
- ____
- ____
- ____
- ____

5 Review:

- ____
- ____
- ____
- ____
- ____

Beautiful things happen when you distance yourself from negative thinking.
Richard AKITA
One life, make it count
RichardAKita
AKitaRichard
www.richardakita.com
image: pixabay.com

Daily fix:

"You will never change your life until you change something you do daily. The secret of your success is found in your daily routine."

2. Your view: _______________________________

____

____

____

3. Daily goals:

- ____
- ____
- ____
- ____
- ____

4. Supporting action:

- ____
- ____
- ____
- ____
- ____

5 Review:

- ____
- ____
- ____
- ____
- ____

Daily fix:

I will not be a poor copy of someone else, whiles God has made me an original brand.

2. Your view: ___________________________

____

____

____

3. Daily goals:

- ___________________________
- ___________________________
- ___________________________
- ___________________________
- ___________________________

4. Supporting action:

- ___________________________
- ___________________________
- ___________________________
- ___________________________
- ___________________________

5 Review:

- ___________________________
- ___________________________
- ___________________________
- ___________________________
- ___________________________

Daily fix:

Born a genius, until I got educated.

2. Your view: _______________________________

____

____

____

3. Daily goals:

- ____

- ____

- ____

- ____

- ____

4. Supporting action:

- ____

- ____

- ____

- ____

- ____

5 Review:

- ____

- ____

- ____

- ____

- ____

Daily fix:

Success is built on a rung of steps.

2. Your view: _______________________________

____

____

____

3. Daily goals:

- ____
- ____
- ____
- ____
- ____

4. Supporting action:

- ____
- ____
- ____
- ____
- ____

5 Review:

- ____
- ____
- ____
- ____
- ____

Daily fix:

Systematisation!!

To scale or go higher these 4 are useful; Escalator, Elevator, Stairs or Ladder. However, when it comes to success, 2 of the 4 are not the best route. Whilst 2 of the 4 gives the opportunity to build on the previous level. WHY?

2. Your view: _______________________________

____

____

____

3. Daily goals:

- _______________________________
- _______________________________
- _______________________________
- _______________________________
- _______________________________

4. Supporting action:

- _______________________________
- _______________________________
- _______________________________
- _______________________________
- _______________________________

5 Review:

- _______________________________
- _______________________________
- _______________________________
- _______________________________
- _______________________________

Daily fix:

There's a word and there's a name that impacts, yet a choice given to man.

2. Your view: ___________________________

____

____

____

3. Daily goals:

- ____
- ____
- ____
- ____
- ____

4. Supporting action:

- ____
- ____
- ____
- ____
- ____

5 Review:

- ____
- ____
- ____
- ____
- ____

Daily fix:

May your diligence produce a tangible result that wil
catapult you beyond your imagination.

2. Your view: _______________________________

____

____

____

3. Daily goals:

- _______________________________________

- _______________________________________

- _______________________________________

- _______________________________________

- _______________________________________

4. Supporting action:

- _______________________________________

- _______________________________________

- _______________________________________

- _______________________________________

- _______________________________________

5 Review:

- _______________________________________

- _______________________________________

- _______________________________________

- _______________________________________

- _______________________________________

Daily fix:

No second, minute, hour, day, week or month is the same, rather in each there is a hidden gem that awaits discovery.

2. Your view: _______________________________

____

____

____

3. Daily goals:

- _______________________________
- _______________________________
- _______________________________
- _______________________________
- _______________________________

4. Supporting action:

- _______________________________
- _______________________________
- _______________________________
- _______________________________
- _______________________________

5 Review:

- _______________________________
- _______________________________
- _______________________________
- _______________________________
- _______________________________

Daily fix:

When awesomeness is attainable, and simplicity is misplaced, the frustration of life is embedded in the mind of the ignorant.

2. Your view: _______________________

____

____

____

3. Daily goals:

- _______________________
- _______________________
- _______________________
- _______________________
- _______________________

4. Supporting action:

- _______________________
- _______________________
- _______________________
- _______________________
- _______________________

5 Review:

- _______________________
- _______________________
- _______________________
- _______________________
- _______________________

Daily fix:

Your impact is so needed so keep stoking the fire of uncomfortableness to waken the giant in your circle of influence.

2. Your view: _______________________________

____

____

____

3. Daily goals:

- ____

- ____

- ____

- ____

- ____

4. Supporting action:

- ____

- ____

- ____

- ____

- ____

5 Review:

- ____

- ____

- ____

- ____

- ____

Daily fix:

Sometimes the promise of tomorrow is enough to see today through, but never neglect the promise of today, because that's what is guaranteed.

2. Your view: _______________________

____

____

____

3. Daily goals:

- _______________________________________

- _______________________________________

- _______________________________________

- _______________________________________

- _______________________________________

4. Supporting action:

- _______________________________________

- _______________________________________

- _______________________________________

- _______________________________________

- _______________________________________

5 Review:

- _______________________________________

- _______________________________________

- _______________________________________

- _______________________________________

- _______________________________________

Daily fix:

The beauty of the day is never hidden but needs discovery. Will you look out for it?

2. Your view: ______________________________

____

____

____

3. Daily goals:

- ______________________________

- ______________________________

- ______________________________

- ______________________________

- ______________________________

4. Supporting action:

- ______________________________

- ______________________________

- ______________________________

- ______________________________

5 Review:

- ______________________________

- ______________________________

- ______________________________

- ______________________________

- ______________________________

Daily fix:

Sweetness is not always found in nectar but in God. May
your experience and discovery of sweetness cause you to
bloom and become contagious.

2. Your view: ___________________________

____

____

____

3. Daily goals:

- ____
- ____
- ____
- ____
- ____

4. Supporting action:

- ____
- ____
- ____
- ____
- ____

5 Review:

- ____
- ____
- ____
- ____
- ____

Daily fix:

Your attitude towards your seed will determine the value you place on your purpose in life.

2. Your view: _______________________________

____

____

____

3. Daily goals:

- ____
- ____
- ____
- ____
- ____

4. Supporting action:

- ____
- ____
- ____
- ____
- ____

5 Review:

- ____
- ____
- ____
- ____
- ____

Daily fix:

The sweetness of knowing is never the answer. But the joy of possessing is sweeter.

2. Your view: ______________________________

____

____

____

3. Daily goals:

- ______________________________
- ______________________________
- ______________________________
- ______________________________
- ______________________________

4. Supporting action:

- ______________________________
- ______________________________
- ______________________________
- ______________________________
- ______________________________

5 Review:

- ______________________________
- ______________________________
- ______________________________
- ______________________________
- ______________________________

Daily fix:

When we focus on our goals, obstacles become stepping stones.

2. Your view: _______________________________

____

____

____

3. Daily goals:

- ____
- ____
- ____
- ____
- ____

4. Supporting action:

- ____
- ____
- ____
- ____
- ____

5 Review:

- ____
- ____
- ____
- ____
- ____

Daily fix:

When you understand your significance, you'll rise to the clarion call. There's nothing ordinary about you. You're endowed with unlimited creative potential, so be the solution in your sphere of influence.

2. Your view: _______________________________

____

____

____

3. Daily goals:

- ____
- ____
- ____
- ____
- ____

4. Supporting action:

- ____
- ____
- ____
- ____
- ____

5 Review:

- ____
- ____
- ____
- ____
- ____

Daily fix:

Your greatest asset is YOU. Anything worth having costs something. What does your commitment to investing in YOU cost? Be willing to pay the price to gain a better YOU. Learn something new today.

2. Your view: _______________________________

____

____

____

3. Daily goals:

- ____
- ____
- ____
- ____
- ____

4. Supporting action:

- ____
- ____
- ____
- ____
- ____

5 Review:

- ____
- ____
- ____
- ____
- ____

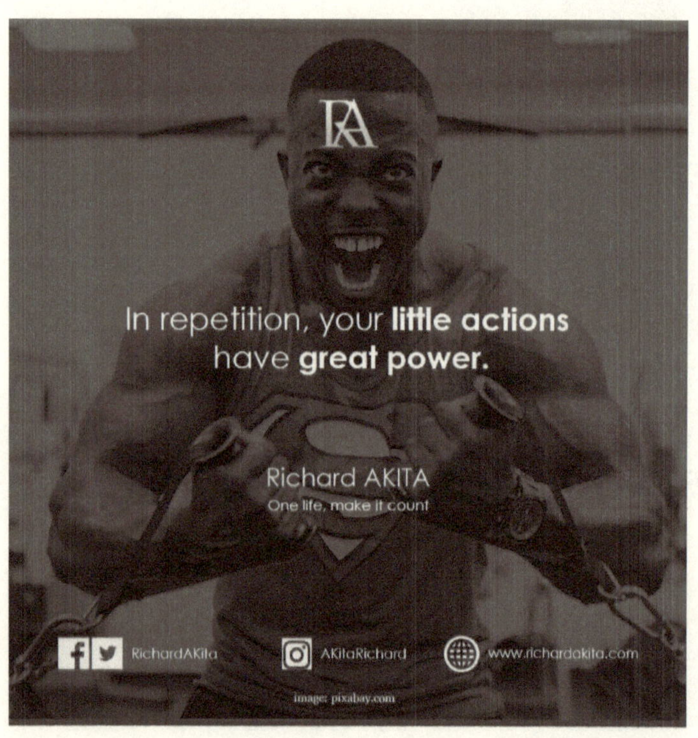

In repetition, your little actions have great power.
Richard AKITA
One life, make it count
RichardAKita
AKitaRichard
www.richardakita.com
image: pixabay.com

Daily fix:

Maximise the moments. Delay can be frustrating yet for the patient it is a season for preparation. *"Because Victory loves preparation"*.

2. Your view: _______________________

____

____

____

3. Daily goals:

- _______________________________________
- _______________________________________
- _______________________________________
- _______________________________________
- _______________________________________

4. Supporting action:

- _______________________________________
- _______________________________________
- _______________________________________
- _______________________________________
- _______________________________________

5 Review:

- _______________________________________
- _______________________________________
- _______________________________________
- _______________________________________
- _______________________________________

Daily fix:

Your beliefs can limit your progress. *"Unbelief blinds people to the truth and robs them of hope"*

2. Your view: _______________________________

____

____

____

3. Daily goals:

- _______________________________________
- _______________________________________
- _______________________________________
- _______________________________________
- _______________________________________

4. Supporting action:

- _______________________________________
- _______________________________________
- _______________________________________
- _______________________________________
- _______________________________________

5 Review:

- _______________________________________
- _______________________________________
- _______________________________________
- _______________________________________
- _______________________________________

Daily fix:

Ditch the doubts and pursue your purpose. Renewing your mind will transform you.

2. Your view: _______________________________

____

____

____

3. Daily goals:

- _______________________________________
- _______________________________________
- _______________________________________
- _______________________________________
- _______________________________________

4. Supporting action:

- _______________________________________
- _______________________________________
- _______________________________________
- _______________________________________
- _______________________________________

5 Review:

- _______________________________________
- _______________________________________
- _______________________________________
- _______________________________________
- _______________________________________

Daily fix:

Incessant foolhardiness erodes confidence.

2. Your view: _______________________

____

____

____

3. Daily goals:

- _______________________________________

- _______________________________________

- _______________________________________

- _______________________________________

- _______________________________________

4. Supporting action:

- _______________________________________

- _______________________________________

- _______________________________________

- _______________________________________

- _______________________________________

5 Review:

- _______________________________________

- _______________________________________

- _______________________________________

- _______________________________________

- _______________________________________

Daily fix:

Life is best lived when you are actively engaged at the helm and not as a spectator. Take responsibility for the life you have and cause a RIPPLE effect of good.

2. Your view: _______________________________

____

____

____

3. Daily goals:

- _______________________________________

- _______________________________________

- _______________________________________

- _______________________________________

- _______________________________________

4. Supporting action:

- _______________________________________

- _______________________________________

- _______________________________________

- _______________________________________

- _______________________________________

5 Review:

- _______________________________________

- _______________________________________

- _______________________________________

- _______________________________________

- _______________________________________

Daily fix:

Why negotiate with Compromise??

2. Your view: _______________________

____

____

____

3. Daily goals:

- _______________________________________
- _______________________________________
- _______________________________________
- _______________________________________
- _______________________________________

4. Supporting action:

- _______________________________________
- _______________________________________
- _______________________________________
- _______________________________________
- _______________________________________

5 Review:

- _______________________________________
- _______________________________________
- _______________________________________
- _______________________________________
- _______________________________________

Daily fix:

Are you living, supporting or spectating?

2. Your view: _______________________________________

____

____

____

3. Daily goals:

- ____
- ____
- ____
- ____
- ____

4. Supporting action:

- ____
- ____
- ____
- ____
- ____

5 Review:

- ____
- ____
- ____
- ____

Daily fix:

Dreams are not fruits on the tree of your life but rather the carrier of a seed that becomes the tree of solution to impact your sphere of influence.

2. **Your view:** _______________________________

____

____

____

3. **Daily goals:**

- _______________________________
- _______________________________
- _______________________________
- _______________________________
- _______________________________

4. **Supporting action:**

- _______________________________
- _______________________________
- _______________________________
- _______________________________
- _______________________________

5 **Review:**

- _______________________________
- _______________________________
- _______________________________
- _______________________________
- _______________________________

Daily fix:

Your history is of no use until it causes a revolution.

2. Your view: _______________________________

____

____

____

3. Daily goals:

- ____
- ____
- ____
- ____
- ____

4. Supporting action:

- ____
- ____
- ____
- ____
- ____

5 Review:

- ____
- ____
- ____
- ____
- ____

Daily fix:

Hardship focuses intensity and passion.

2. Your view: _______________________________

____

____

____

3. Daily goals:

- ____

- ____

- ____

- ____

- ____

4. Supporting action:

- ____

- ____

- ____

- ____

- ____

5 Review:

- ____

- ____

- ____

- ____

- ____

Daily fix:

Little drops of water make a mighty ocean.
Anything worth having cost something. What does your
commitment to investing in YOU cost?

2. Your view: _______________________________

____

____

____

3. Daily goals:

- ____

- ____

- ____

- ____

- ____

4. Supporting action:

- ____

- ____

- ____

- ____

- ____

5 Review:

- ____

- ____

- ____

- ____

- ____

• • •

Daily fix:

The opulence of the mind must be expressed.

2. Your view: _______________________

____

____

____

3. Daily goals:

- _____________________________________

- _____________________________________

- _____________________________________

- _____________________________________

- _____________________________________

4. Supporting action:

- _____________________________________

- _____________________________________

- _____________________________________

- _____________________________________

- _____________________________________

5 Review:

- _____________________________________

- _____________________________________

- _____________________________________

- _____________________________________

- _____________________________________

Daily fix:

Be thankful for each new challenge, because it will build your strength and character. Your attitude makes the difference.

2. Your view: _______________________________

____

____

____

3. Daily goals:

- ____

- ____

- ____

- ____

- ____

4. Supporting action:

- ____

- ____

- ____

- ____

- ____

5 Review:

- ____

- ____

- ____

- ____

- ____

• • •

Daily fix:

You failed so what? Forgive yourself and create the future you desire by leveraging the lessons from fear, failure and defeat.

2. Your view: _______________________________

____

____

____

3. Daily goals:

- _______________________________________
- _______________________________________
- _______________________________________
- _______________________________________
- _______________________________________

4. Supporting action:

- _______________________________________
- _______________________________________
- _______________________________________
- _______________________________________
- _______________________________________

5 Review:

- _______________________________________
- _______________________________________
- _______________________________________
- _______________________________________
- _______________________________________

Daily fix:

Step up!! Either it's young age or ageing younger.
But on reflection see how you have permitted failure,
fear and defeat shape your future.

2. Your view: _______________________________

____

____

____

3. Daily goals:

- ____

- ____

- ____

- ____

- ____

4. Supporting action:

- ____

- ____

- ____

- ____

- ____

5 Review:

- ____

- ____

- ____

- ____

- ____

Daily fix:

True fulfilment is not just about doing what you are good at: NO! True fulfilment lies in doing what you are EXCEPTIONALLY good at!!!

2. Your view: ___________________________

____

____

____

3. Daily goals:

- ___________________________
- ___________________________
- ___________________________
- ___________________________
- ___________________________

4. Supporting action:

- ___________________________
- ___________________________
- ___________________________
- ___________________________
- ___________________________

5 Review:

- ___________________________
- ___________________________
- ___________________________
- ___________________________
- ___________________________

Daily fix:

Who, but only you can determine your destination.

Do not let others opinion of you define who you are. A driver determines their destination and not the vehicle. Are you in the driver's seat?

2. Your view: _______________________________

____

____

____

3. Daily goals:

- _______________________________
- _______________________________
- _______________________________
- _______________________________
- _______________________________

4. Supporting action:

- _______________________________
- _______________________________
- _______________________________
- _______________________________
- _______________________________

5 Review:

- _______________________________
- _______________________________
- _______________________________
- _______________________________

Daily fix:

There are two types of Pain in this world: Pain that hurts you, and Pain that changes you!

2. Your view: _______________________________

____

____

____

3. Daily goals:

- ____

- ____

- ____

- ____

- ____

4. Supporting action:

- ____

- ____

- ____

- ____

- ____

5 Review:

- ____

- ____

- ____

- ____

- ____

The difference between TRY
and TRIUMPH is a little

oomph.

Richard AKITA
One life, make it count.

 RichardAKita
 RichardAKita
 RichardAKita

Daily fix:

Never judge yourself through the lens of others opinion.

2. Your view: _______________________________

____

____

____

3. Daily goals:

- _______________________________________
- _______________________________________
- _______________________________________
- _______________________________________
- _______________________________________

4. Supporting action:

- _______________________________________
- _______________________________________
- _______________________________________
- _______________________________________
- _______________________________________

5 Review:

- _______________________________________
- _______________________________________
- _______________________________________
- _______________________________________
- _______________________________________

Daily fix:

What sound are you listening to?
The sound of victory is quieter than the noise of failure, yet it
is failure that announces victory.

2. Your view: _______________________________

____

____

____

3. Daily goals:

- ____

- ____

- ____

- ____

- ____

4. Supporting action:

- ____

- ____

- ____

- ____

- ____

5 Review:

- ____

- ____

- ____

- ____

- ____

Daily fix:

What are you focusing on?

Every encounter in your life will leave a memory. Your job is to focus on the memory that propels you forward, energises you to dream bigger and live your purpose. For whatever memory you focus on grows.

2. Your view: _______________________________

____

____

____

3. Daily goals:

- ____
- ____
- ____
- ____
- ____

4. Supporting action:

- ____
- ____
- ____
- ____
- ____

5 Review:

- ____
- ____
- ____
- ____
- ____

Daily fix:

Speak victory in the face of adversity, speak love in the moments of hatred and speak encouraging lexis into your live. Live your harvested seeds.

2. Your view: ________________________________

____

____

____

3. Daily goals:

- ________________________________
- ________________________________
- ________________________________
- ________________________________
- ________________________________

4. Supporting action:

- ________________________________
- ________________________________
- ________________________________
- ________________________________
- ________________________________

5 Review:

- ________________________________
- ________________________________
- ________________________________
- ________________________________
- ________________________________

Daily fix:

What are you saying?
Every word uttered is a seed. What harvest do you desire?
A careless word can frustrate and stunt your progress.

2. Your view: _______________________________

____

____

____

3. Daily goals:

- ____

- ____

- ____

- ____

- ____

4. Supporting action:

- ____

- ____

- ____

- ____

- ____

5 Review:

- ____

- ____

- ____

- ____

- ____

Daily fix:

Face your past without regret. Handle your present with confidence. Prepare for the future without fear. Keep the faith and drop the fear.

2. Your view: _______________________________

____

____

____

3. Daily goals:

- ____
- ____
- ____
- ____
- ____

4. Supporting action:

- ____
- ____
- ____
- ____
- ____

5 Review:

- ____
- ____
- ____
- ____
- ____

Daily fix:

Here's a thought that's bugging me
Who is in control?
The opinion of others or your opinion of yourself?

2. Your view: ______________________________

____

____

____

3. Daily goals:

- ____

- ____

- ____

- ____

- ____

4. Supporting action:

- ____

- ____

- ____

- ____

- ____

5 Review:

- ____

- ____

- ____

- ____

Daily fix:

It's all is the maths.
Who is influencing you? Your friends, community, business, family or education?
Critically evaluate their contribution in your life, are they adding, multiplying, dividing or subtracting? Go on do the math.

2. Your view: ___________________________________

____

____

____

3. Daily goals:

- ___________________________________
- ___________________________________
- ___________________________________
- ___________________________________
- ___________________________________

4. Supporting action:

- ___________________________________
- ___________________________________
- ___________________________________
- ___________________________________
- ___________________________________

5 Review:

- ___________________________________
- ___________________________________
- ___________________________________
- ___________________________________
- ___________________________________

Daily fix:

One life, one race, one you!

The slow movement of a lion doesn't show weakness or tiredness but rather a calculated step to get its prey. Stay in your track and keep your focus on your goal.

2. Your view: ___________________________________

____

____

____

3. Daily goals:

- ___________________________________
- ___________________________________
- ___________________________________
- ___________________________________
- ___________________________________

4. Supporting action:

- ___________________________________
- ___________________________________
- ___________________________________
- ___________________________________
- ___________________________________

5 Review:

- ___________________________________
- ___________________________________
- ___________________________________
- ___________________________________
- ___________________________________

Daily fix:

Thinking is the ultimate human resource.

2. Your view: _______________________________

____

____

____

3. Daily goals:

- ____

- ____

- ____

- ____

- ____

4. Supporting action:

- ____

- ____

- ____

- ____

- ____

5 Review:

- ____

- ____

- ____

- ____

- ____

Daily fix:

Identity crisis!!
Puzzle pieces when alone are useless but when assembled not only
completes but shows off the value and beauty of the puzzle. Yet the
puzzle piece doesn't know its value.
What's your value?

2. Your view: ____

____

____

____

3. Daily goals:

- ____
- ____
- ____
- ____
- ____

4. Supporting action:

- ____
- ____
- ____
- ____
- ____

5 Review:

- ____
- ____
- ____
- ____
- ____

Daily fix:

Winter never apologizes for being cold. Therefore, do not apologize for being you.

2. Your view: _______________________________

____

____

____

3. Daily goals:

- ____
- ____
- ____
- ____
- ____

4. Supporting action:

- ____
- ____
- ____
- ____
- ____

5 Review:

- ____
- ____
- ____
- ____
- ____

Daily fix:

I am Incredible, I am Strong, nothing Fazes ME. Yes, that's ME.

2. Your view: ______________________________

____

____

____

3. Daily goals:

- ______________________________
- ______________________________
- ______________________________
- ______________________________
- ______________________________

4. Supporting action:

- ______________________________
- ______________________________
- ______________________________
- ______________________________
- ______________________________

5 Review:

- ______________________________
- ______________________________
- ______________________________
- ______________________________
- ______________________________

Daily fix:

Change!

Times change, we change, situations around us change and people change but there is one constant HOPE! Let your hope fuel your faith. Embrace change to be the best.

2. Your view: ___________________________________

____

____

____

3. Daily goals:

- ___________________________________
- ___________________________________
- ___________________________________
- ___________________________________
- ___________________________________

4. Supporting action:

- ___________________________________
- ___________________________________
- ___________________________________
- ___________________________________
- ___________________________________

5 Review:

- ___________________________________
- ___________________________________
- ___________________________________
- ___________________________________
- ___________________________________

Daily fix:

Stiff arrogance is the hallmark of stupidity

2. Your view: _______________________________

____

____

____

3. Daily goals:

- _______________________________________

- _______________________________________

- _______________________________________

- _______________________________________

- _______________________________________

4. Supporting action:

- _______________________________________

- _______________________________________

- _______________________________________

- _______________________________________

- _______________________________________

5 Review:

- _______________________________________

- _______________________________________

- _______________________________________

- _______________________________________

- _______________________________________

Daily fix:

At all times, we must keep open the possibility that much more is possible ~ Bofy Idiodi

2. Your view: _________________________________

____

____

____

3. Daily goals:

- ____
- ____
- ____
- ____
- ____

4. Supporting action:

- ____
- ____
- ____
- ____
- ____

5 Review:

- ____
- ____
- ____
- ____
- ____

Daily fix:

Be a change agent!

Youth is no barrier to strength and wisdom is not exclusive to the aged. Both manifest through development and available to all. Add value and impact a life today.

2. Your view: _______________________________

____

____

____

3. Daily goals:

- ____

- ____

- ____

- ____

- ____

4. Supporting action:

- ____

- ____

- ____

- ____

- ____

5 Review:

- ____

- ____

- ____

- ____

- ____

Daily fix:

Watch your diet!! Hands create, eyes assess and feet travel. But the brain navigates. What are you feeding your brain?

2. Your view: _______________________

____

____

____

3. Daily goals:

- _______________________
- _______________________
- _______________________
- _______________________
- _______________________

4. Supporting action:

- _______________________
- _______________________
- _______________________
- _______________________
- _______________________

5 Review:

- _______________________
- _______________________
- _______________________
- _______________________
- _______________________

Daily fix:

"Our greatest weakness lies in giving up. The most certain way to succeed is always to try just one more time." – Thomas Edison

2. Your view: _______________________________

____

____

____

3. Daily goals:

- ____
- ____
- ____
- ____
- ____

4. Supporting action:

- ____
- ____
- ____
- ____
- ____

5 Review:

- ____
- ____
- ____
- ____
- ____

Daily fix:

Success and failure are just pitstops in life's journey.

2. Your view: _______________________________

____

____

____

3. Daily goals:

- ____

- ____

- ____

- ____

- ____

4. Supporting action:

- ____

- ____

- ____

- ____

- ____

5 Review:

- ____

- ____

- ____

- ____

- ____

Daily fix:

Introspection!!
What ADDS to you?
What MULTIPLIES your effort?
What DIVIDES your attention?
What TAKES away your desire?
The solution is your CHOICE.

2. Your view: _______________________________________

____

____

____

3. Daily goals:

- ____

- ____

- ____

- ____

- ____

4. Supporting action:

- ____

- ____

- ____

- ____

- ____

5 Review:

- ____

- ____

- ____

- ____

- ____

Daily fix:

Every behaviour has a positive intention.

2. Your view: ______________________

____

____

____

3. Daily goals:

- ______________________
- ______________________
- ______________________
- ______________________
- ______________________

4. Supporting action:

- ______________________
- ______________________
- ______________________
- ______________________
- ______________________

5 Review:

- ______________________
- ______________________
- ______________________
- ______________________
- ______________________

Daily fix:

Self-assessment!

What's your worth?

2. Your view: _______________________________

____

____

____

3. Daily goals:

- ______________________________________
- ______________________________________
- ______________________________________
- ______________________________________
- ______________________________________

4. Supporting action:

- ______________________________________
- ______________________________________
- ______________________________________
- ______________________________________
- ______________________________________

5 Review:

- ______________________________________
- ______________________________________
- ______________________________________
- ______________________________________
- ______________________________________

Daily fix:

What gets you started is desire, what keeps you going is desire and this same desire ensures you safely arrive at your destination. Start your day by ending your day.

2. Your view: _______________________

____

____

____

3. Daily goals:

- _______________________
- _______________________
- _______________________
- _______________________
- _______________________

4. Supporting action:

- _______________________
- _______________________
- _______________________
- _______________________
- _______________________

5 Review:

- _______________________
- _______________________
- _______________________
- _______________________
- _______________________

Daily fix:

You're unstoppable! It's not what people say about you that defeats you. Rather it's what you say and think about yourself that brings your defeat.

2. Your view: _______________________

____

____

____

3. Daily goals:

- _______________________
- _______________________
- _______________________
- _______________________
- _______________________

4. Supporting action:

- _______________________
- _______________________
- _______________________
- _______________________
- _______________________

5 Review:

- _______________________
- _______________________
- _______________________
- _______________________
- _______________________

Daily fix:

Who's in control?

Deliberate choices don't guarantee complete control.

2. Your view: _______________________________

____

____

____

3. Daily goals:

- _______________________________
- _______________________________
- _______________________________
- _______________________________
- _______________________________

4. Supporting action:

- _______________________________
- _______________________________
- _______________________________
- _______________________________
- _______________________________

5 Review:

- _______________________________
- _______________________________
- _______________________________
- _______________________________
- _______________________________

Daily fix:

Retrospection!!
I often wonder why toddlers when mastering walking, laugh when
they fall in their attempts yet immediately get up and try again.
However, adults cry, retreat and complain bitterly when they fail.
Have we got it all wrong?

2. Your view: _______________________________
____
____
____

3. Daily goals:

- ____
- ____
- ____
- ____
- ____

4. Supporting action:

- ____
- ____
- ____
- ____
- ____

5 Review:

- ____
- ____
- ____
- ____
- ____

Daily fix:

Evaluating your year!
What's your best victory?
What's your worst failure?
What's your biggest dream?
What's your smallest irritant?
Your success is your responsibility.

2. Your view: ______________________________

____

____

____

3. Daily goals:

- ______________________________
- ______________________________
- ______________________________
- ______________________________
- ______________________________

4. Supporting action:

- ______________________________
- ______________________________
- ______________________________
- ______________________________
- ______________________________

5 Review:

- ______________________________
- ______________________________
- ______________________________
- ______________________________
- ______________________________

Daily fix:

Reactions!!

Our emotions can either be a hindrance or a hydrant.
Both have their uses but what triggers yours?
However, does being calm show strength?
It's a conundrum

2. Your view: _______________________________

____

____

____

3. Daily goals:

- _______________________________________

- _______________________________________

- _______________________________________

- _______________________________________

- _______________________________________

4. Supporting action:

- _______________________________________

- _______________________________________

- _______________________________________

- _______________________________________

- _______________________________________

5 Review:

- _______________________________________

- _______________________________________

- _______________________________________

- _______________________________________

- _______________________________________

Daily fix:

Leveraging your Weakness!

Don't shy from acknowledging your weakness, as it the key to tapping into grace.

For in our weakness God's power is perfected.

2. Your view: _______________________________

____

____

____

3. Daily goals:

-   _______________________________________
-   _______________________________________
-   _______________________________________
-   _______________________________________
-   _______________________________________

4. Supporting action:

-   _______________________________________
-   _______________________________________
-   _______________________________________
-   _______________________________________
-   _______________________________________

5 Review:

-   _______________________________________
-   _______________________________________
-   _______________________________________
-   _______________________________________
-   _______________________________________

Daily fix:

The human capital is never bankrupt.

2. Your view: ____________________________________

____

____

____

3. Daily goals:

- ____
- ____
- ____
- ____
- ____

4. Supporting action:

- ____
- ____
- ____
- ____
- ____

5 Review:

- ____
- ____
- ____
- ____
- ____

Daily fix:

Size matters!!
All the bread dough need is a small yeast to make it rise.
The deadliest of insects that kills 27 million people a year is the mosquito.
Small is powerful.
What small habits are you feeding?

2. Your view: ___________________________

____

____

____

3. Daily goals:

- ___________________________
- ___________________________
- ___________________________
- ___________________________
- ___________________________

4. Supporting action:

- ___________________________
- ___________________________
- ___________________________
- ___________________________
- ___________________________

5 Review:

- ___________________________
- ___________________________
- ___________________________
- ___________________________
- ___________________________

Daily fix:

You cannot change what you refuse to confront.

2. Your view: ___________________________________

____

____

____

3. Daily goals:

- ____
- ____
- ____
- ____
- ____

4. Supporting action:

- ____
- ____
- ____
- ____
- ____

5 Review:

- ____
- ____
- ____
- ____
- ____

Daily fix:

Everything is subject to change!
Patterns are blueprints
Patterns are habitual
Patterns are influenced
But patterns are not rigid.
So, if you don't like what you see, just erase and start all over.

2. Your view: ____

____

____

____

3. Daily goals:

- ____
- ____
- ____
- ____
- ____

4. Supporting action:

- ____
- ____
- ____
- ____
- ____

5 Review:

- ____
- ____
- ____
- ____
- ____

Daily fix:

Sometimes you need to distance yourself to see things clearly

Sometimes good things fall apart so better things can fall together.

2. Your view: ________________________

____

____

____

3. Daily goals:

- ____________________________________
- ____________________________________
- ____________________________________
- ____________________________________
- ____________________________________

4. Supporting action:

- ____________________________________
- ____________________________________
- ____________________________________
- ____________________________________
- ____________________________________

5 Review:

- ____________________________________
- ____________________________________
- ____________________________________
- ____________________________________
- ____________________________________

Daily fix:

Disrespect time, miss opportunity.

2. Your view: _______________________

____

____

____

3. Daily goals:

- _____________________________________

- _____________________________________

- _____________________________________

- _____________________________________

- _____________________________________

4. Supporting action:

- _____________________________________

- _____________________________________

- _____________________________________

- _____________________________________

- _____________________________________

5 Review:

- _____________________________________

- _____________________________________

- _____________________________________

- _____________________________________

- _____________________________________

Daily fix:

All Change!!

The truth never deceives.
Paradoxically when confronted with the truth, we vehemently end up convincing ourselves it's deception.
Acknowledge the truth and apply change where needed.

2. Your view: _______________________________________

____

____

____

3. Daily goals:

- _______________________________________
- _______________________________________
- _______________________________________
- _______________________________________
- _______________________________________

4. Supporting action:

- _______________________________________
- _______________________________________
- _______________________________________
- _______________________________________
- _______________________________________

5 Review:

- _______________________________________
- _______________________________________
- _______________________________________
- _______________________________________
- _______________________________________

9 789988 292515